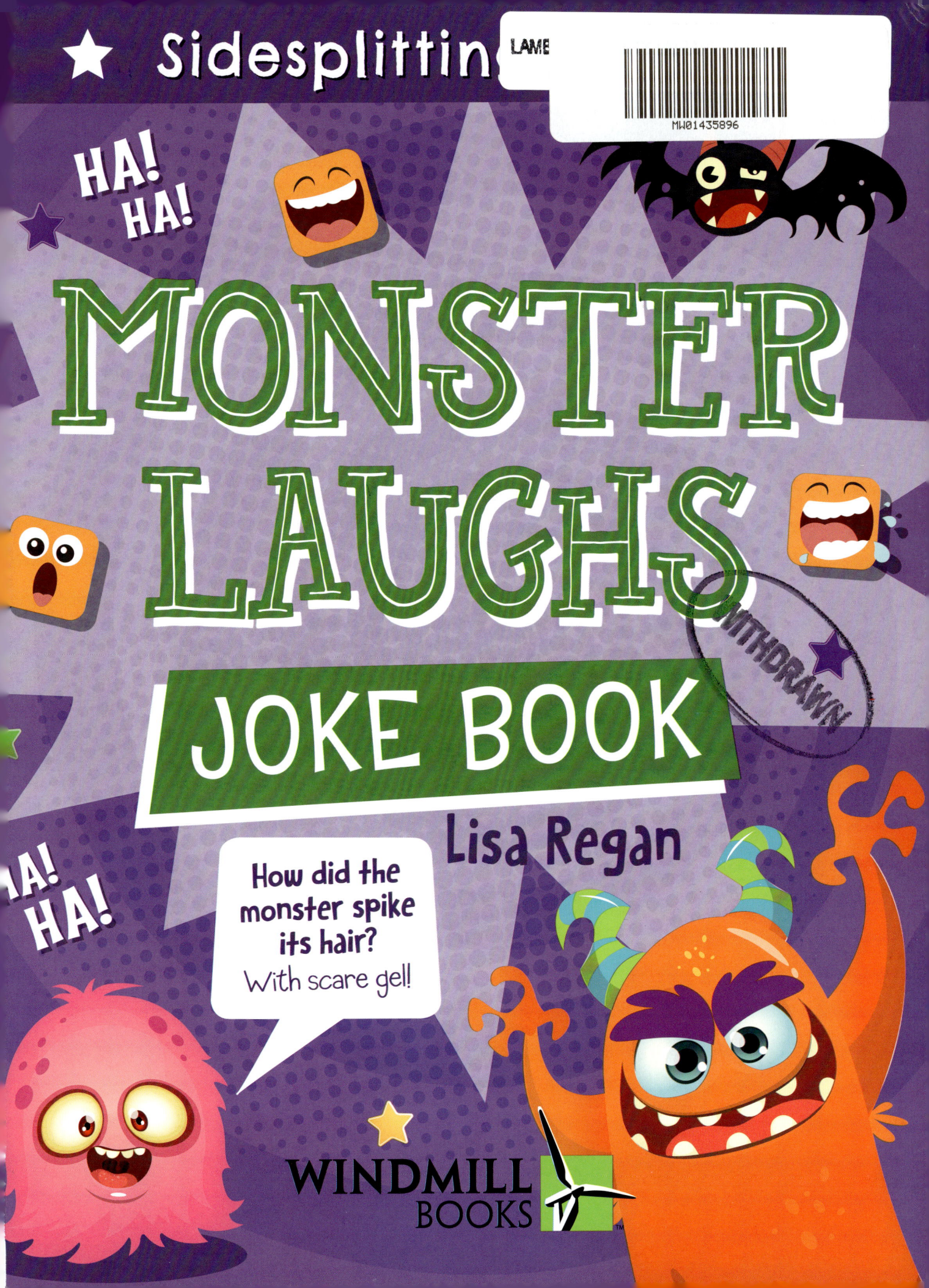

★ Sidesplitting

MONSTER LAUGHS

JOKE BOOK

Lisa Regan

How did the monster spike its hair? With scare gel!

HA! HA!

WINDMILL BOOKS

Published in 2020 by Windmill Books,
an Imprint of Rosen Publishing
29 East 21st Street, New York, NY 10010

Copyright © Arcturus Holdings Ltd, 2020

All rights reserved. No part of this book may be reproduced in any form without permission in writing from the publisher, except by a reviewer.

Cataloging-in-Publication Data

Names: Regan, Lisa.
Title: Monster laughs joke book / Lisa Regan.
Description: New York : Windmill Books, 2020. | Series: Sidesplitting jokes | Includes glossary and index.
Identifiers: ISBN 9781725395985 (pbk.) | ISBN 9781725396005 (library bound) | ISBN 9781725395992 (6 pack)
Subjects: LCSH: Monsters--Juvenile humor. | Wit and humor, Juvenile.
Classification: LCC PN6231.M665 R465 2020 | DDC 808.8'037--dc23

Manufactured in the United States of America

CPSIA Compliance Information: Batch BW20WM: For further information contact
Rosen Publishing, New York, New York at 1-800-237-9932

WARNING!

This book is dangerously funny!

Are you ready for the best selection of funny stuff ever gathered together under one cover? Prepare yourself for a heap of brand new jokes, a pile of classic sidesplitters, and a big bundle of laughs. It all adds up to a stack of fun to share with your friends and family. Warn them to find a safe place to listen, as they'll soon be laughing their heads off!

HA HA HAA

What sort of monsters work in graveyards?

A skeleton staff!

How does a monster see its future?

It reads its horrorscope.

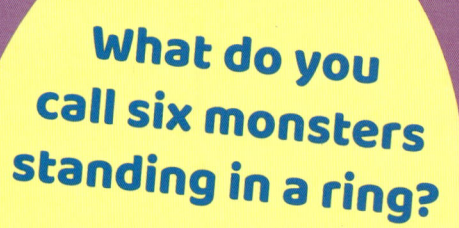

What do you call six monsters standing in a ring?

A vicious circle!

How do you know when there's a scary monster under your bed?

You don't— that's what makes it scary!

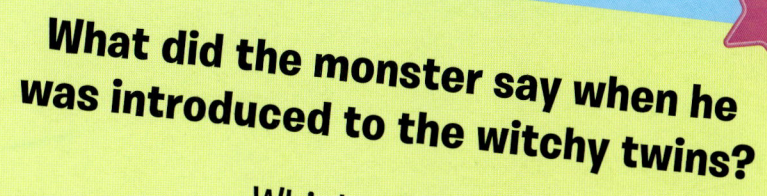

What did the monster say when he was introduced to the witchy twins?

Which is witch?

How do monsters stay cool?

With scare conditioning!

What do Italian monsters eat?

Spook-ghetti!

Why do monsters go dancing?

To meet up with the boogyman.

Where do you mostly find zombies in the city?

Dead ends.

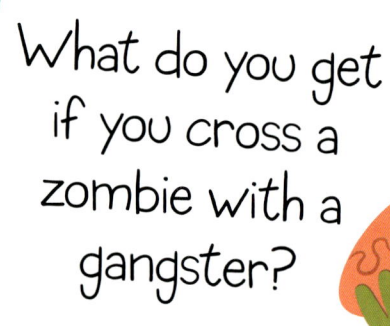

What do you get if you cross a zombie with a gangster?

Frankenstein's mobster!

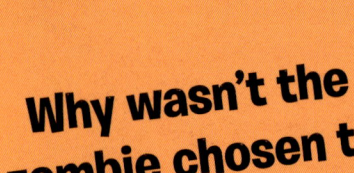

Why wasn't the zombie chosen to teach at drama school?

They wanted someone more lively!

What is a zombie most likely to receive a medal for?

Dead-ication!

What game do zombies like playing?

Hide-and-shriek!

Why are there no great zombie authors?

Because dead men tell no tales.

How did the zombie describe her boyfriend?

Drop-dead gorgeous!

What do you call zombie twins?

Dead ringers!

What's a vampire's best day of the year?
Fangs—giving.

Why does Dracula wear shiny black shoes?
Because flip-flops look stupid with his suit.

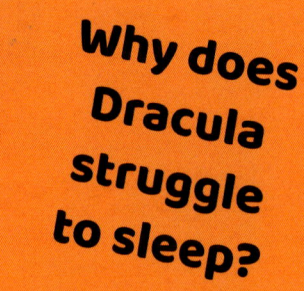

Why does Dracula struggle to sleep?
Because of his coffin.

What did the vampire say about his dog?
Don't worry, he's all bite and no bark.

What kind of blood do pessimistic vampires like best?

B negative!

Which ice cream do vampires like best?

Vein-illa.

What did the vampire say when he'd drunk enough blood?

No more, fang you.

Where does Dracula visit first when he's in New York City?

The Vampire State Building.

Why did the banshee marry a pirate?

So she could wail the seven seas.

What music do mummies like best?

Wrap music!

When does a banshee eat breakfast?

In the moaning.

Why don't mummies go on vacation?

They're afraid they'll relax and unwind!

Why couldn't the mummy make any friends?

He was too wrapped up in himself!

Why can you trust a mummy with your secrets?

They're good at keeping things under wraps!

Why are banshees good tennis partners?

They make a fine old racket.

What dessert do banshees usually order?

I scream.

Why shouldn't you ride a broom if you're in a bad mood?

You might fly off the handle!

Why did the skeleton go to a family gathering?

To meet up with its flesh and blood!

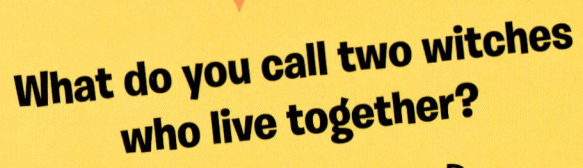

What do you call two witches who live together?

Broom-mates!

Why don't skeletons like gusty weather?

It goes right through them!

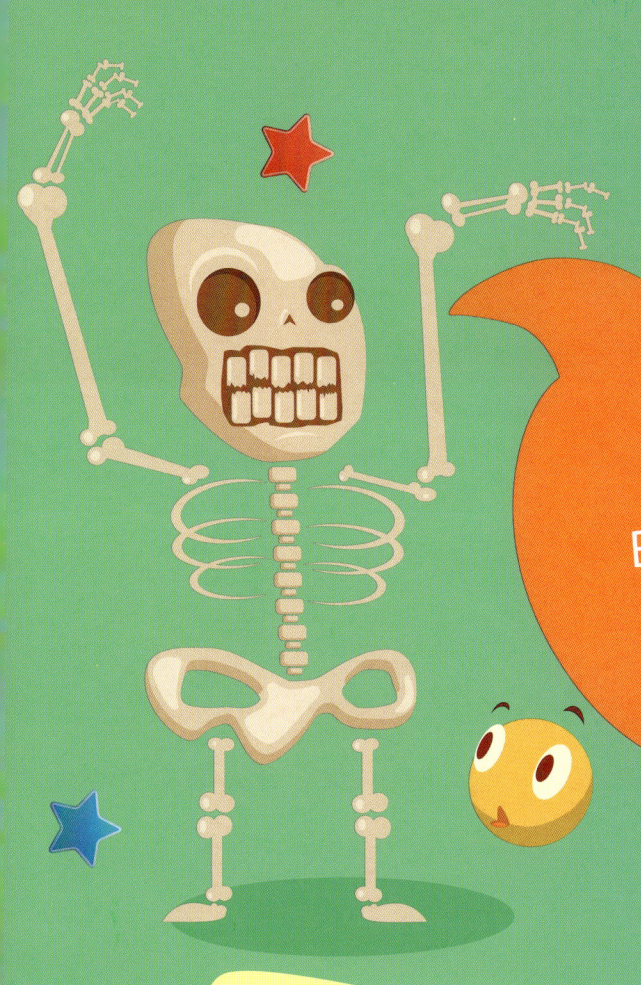

Why don't skeletons get angry?

Because nothing gets under their skin!

What does a witch do on her birthday?

She has a spell-ebration!

Where does a witch park?

In the broom closet.

What did the skeleton's family say when it stayed out in the snow all night?

You numbskull!

Where do baby monsters go while their parents work?

Dayscare.

Did you hear about the monster that ate a lamp?

It just wanted a light lunch.

What does a monster say at the start of a meal?

Bone appetit!

What's big and hairy and goes beep beep?

A monster stuck in traffic.

Why did the monster go to see the nurse?

He felt abominable, yeti didn't know why.

How did the monster spike its hair?

With scare gel.

How can you tell if a monster has a false eye?

It might come out in conversation.

Why did the monster get a top score in the test?

Because two heads are better than one.

What does a vampire never order at a restaurant?

A stake sandwich!

When are you most likely to see a vampire?

In the dead of night!

Why did the vampire teacher suddenly leave class?

She had a coffin fit!

Why do vampires like red pens?

So they can draw blood!

A werewolf and Dracula had a fight. Who won?

The werewolf, because Dracula sucks.

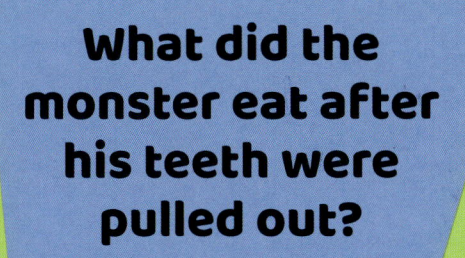

What did the monster eat after his teeth were pulled out?

The dentist.

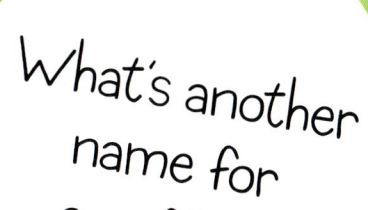

What's another name for a coffin?

Dead wood.

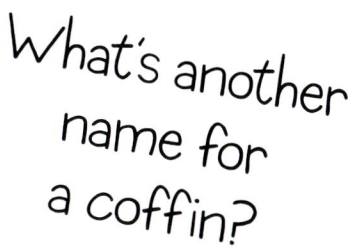

How does Dracula feel after a long night?

Dead on his feet!

What did the huge, clumsy ghost do?

Made a giant boo-boo!

What did the mother ghost say to her kids before driving them home?

Fasten your sheet belts.

What did the ghost say as it floated across the room?

Just passing through!

Did you hear about the frozen ghost?

People were scared stiff.

Why don't ghosts do stand-up comedy?

In case they get booed off the stage.

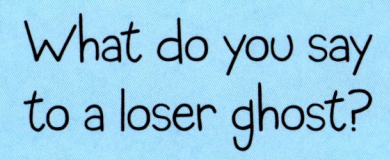

What do you say to a loser ghost?

Get a life!

Which tourist attraction is the most haunted?

Death Valley.

Did you hear about the ghost that got lost in the fog?

He was mist.

What did the evil monster say when she had twins?

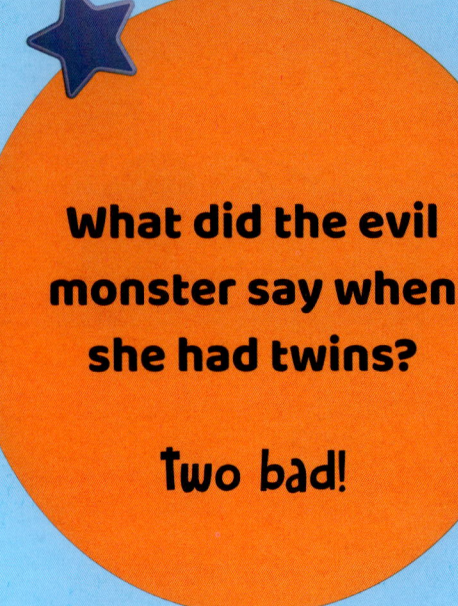

Two bad!

How do monsters like their eggs?

Terror-fried!

What goes "Ha, ha, thunk"?

A monster laughing its head off!

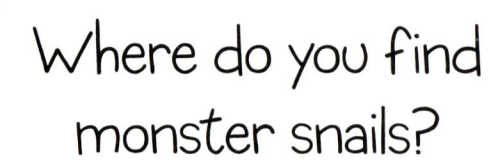

Where do you find monster snails?

On the end of monsters' fingers.

What do baby monsters like before they sleep?

A bite-time story.

Why don't evil monsters have bedrooms?

Because there's no rest for the wicked!

What does a yeti say when it's trying to explain something?

Do you get my drift?

How many monsters are good at mathematics?

None, unless you Count Dracula.

What do you say as you stake a vampire in the heart?

So long, sucker!

Why do they put fences around cemeteries?

Because people are dying to get in!

Where should you hide if a zombie is chasing you?

The living room!

What do you call a troll with a bad leg?

A hobblin' goblin.

Why do Frankenstein's monster's arms squeak?

Because he ran out of elbow grease!

Glossary

banshee In folk stories, a female spirit who warns that someone is about to die by giving a long, sad cry.

goblin In fairy tales, a small, ugly creature that enjoys causing trouble.

pessimistic Having the attitude that bad things are going to happen.

yeti Another word for Abominable Snowman.

zombies In horror stories, zombies are dead people who have been brought back to life.

Index

B
babies 14, 21
banshees 10, 11
beds 4, 21
blood 9, 12, 16

C
cemeteries 22
coffins 16, 17

D
dancing 5
Dracula 8, 9, 17, 21

F
Frankenstein 6, 23

G
ghosts 18, 19
goblins 22
graveyards 4

M
mathematics 21
meals 14, 16
mummies 10, 11

S
school 6, 16
skeletons 4, 12, 13
snails 20
steak 16
stories 21

T
teachers 16
twins 5, 7, 20

V
vampires 8, 9, 16, 22

W
werewolves 17
witches 12, 13

Y
yeti 21

Z
zombies 6, 7, 22

24